I HATE MY SON-IN-LAW

I HATE MY SON-IN-LAW

100 Ways I Got *Silent* Revenge

Harry Ketsu
and
Hagoromo Tennyo

Simple Logic Publications

I HATE MY SON-IN-LAW

Copyright © 2019 Simple Logic Publications. All rights reserved. No part of this book may be reproduced or transmitted by any means or in any form without the prior written consent from the authors or publisher. This includes photocopying, scanning, transmitting by or storing in any computer-based device or system.

Disclaimer: This book has been created for the purpose of entertainment only. The authors and publisher make no representations or warranties of any kind with respect to this book or its contents. The authors and publisher and any of its employees disclaim any and all liability for any damages arising out of or in connection with this book. This includes, but is not limited to, distress, offense, insult, injury or any damage whatsoever to any current or future relationships. Any use of this book or its content is at the reader's own risk. Please read more on page 5.

ISBN 978-0-9954007-1-9 (Trade Paperback)

For information, please contact:
harryketsu@simplelogicpublications.com

Please note that we do not accept unsolicited manuscripts.

Illustration under license from
shutterstock.com and istockphoto.com

Printed in Australia • United Kingdom
• United States of America

Table of Contents

INTRODUCTION 1

PART 1
Keeping Him Clean

His Toothbrush 9
His Toothbrush 2 10
Bath-Towel 11
Shampoo 12
Shampoo 2 13
Comb and Brush 14
Comb and Brush 2 15
His Soap 16
His Toothpaste 17
Smelling Good 18

PART 2
His Car

Tires 21
Driver's Seat 22
Driver's Seat 2 23
More Driver's Seat 24
Feel Like Barfing 25

Feel Like Barfing 2	26
Dog Poop	27
More Dog Poop	28
Windshield	29
Bumper Sticker	30

PART 3
Clothes Make the Man

Pocket Surprise	33
Wiggle Room	34
Gum	35
Darn Laces	36
Itching Powder	37
Helping Hand	38
Fat Head	39
Your Scent	40
Super Glue	41
His Favorite Pants	42
Use for Cockroaches	43
What a Heel	44
Garden Creatures	45
Hammer and Nail	46
Insoles	47
His Favorite Shirts	48

PART 4

Get Him Where He Lives

Toilet Seat Fun 51

More Toilet Seat Fun 52

Peeing 53

Farting 54

No Shave Today 55

Toilet Paper 56

Laxatives 57

Big Poop 58

Pillow Case 59

His Side of the Bed 60

His Underwear 61

His Ugly Face 62

Beer and Soda 63

Beer and Soda 2 64

Cactus Cooler 65

Bugs 66

Hair Wad 67

Toilet Fun 68

More Toilet Fun 69

Good Night Boy 70

Make Him Sick 71

Make Him Miserable 72

PART 5

Get Him Where He Works

Cheap Cologne	75
Leaky Pen	76
Junk Mail	77
Body Odor	78
Booze It Up	79
Prank Calls	80
A Good Reference	81
Getting Personal	82
More Phone Calls	83
Unexpected Visit	84
New Ideas	85
Late to Work	86
Impressing the Boss	87
Chewed Gum	88

PART 6

Embarrass and Inconvenience Him

Fart and Blame	91
Wakey Wakey	92
More Wakey Wakey	93
No More TV	94
Free Phones	95
Dinner With Family	96
Phone Calls and Email	97

Sell His Car	98
Sales People	99
Personal Question Time	100
No Phone	101
Junk	102

PART 7
Trouble With The Wife

Inflatable Sex Doll	105
Porn DVDs	106
Dating Sites	107
Love Letter	108
Cross Dressing	109
Nudie Magazines	110
Late Night Call	111
Magazine Subscriptions	112
Rubber Sex Toy	113
Flowers For Him	114
His Computer	115
Valentine's Day	116
Old Lovers	117
Mystery Girl	118
Whose Bra?	119
Not My Lipstick	120
EPILOGUE	121

Introduction

Maybe it seems like only a few years ago when your daughter was playing with dolls. It might seem like it wasn't that long ago since you attended her piano or dance recitals. And maybe it seems like it was only yesterday when you helped her pick out the dress she wore to her high school prom.

You may have likely started making plans for your daughter the day she was born. You might have thought about where she would attend school. Maybe you had hoped and planned for her to attend a particular college or university. It might be that you hoped she would become a teacher, lawyer or doctor. And you certainly must have thought about, even dreamed about, the day your daughter would find that perfect man, the man whom you would be proud of – your Son-in-Law.

That big day finally comes. Your daughter gets married. But to your horror, disapproval and disappointment, your daughter married a loser, an idiot, a real dickhead/wanker, someone you truly despise. From that day forward, you may had thought all was lost, that there was nothing you could do.

This happened to me and that's what I thought.

Not one to give up, over the months and years that followed, I thought about and wrote down *things* I could do that could enable me to get my revenge. (My full list is revealed in this book.)

I knew the 100 things in this book were unlikely to change my son-in-law. Chances are he will never be the son-in-law of my dreams. But by carrying out the things in this book, I felt ~~a little~~ a lot better: I felt a sense of justice.

My aim was not to set out to injury or kill my son-in-law. Nor was it meant to put him (or me) in jail for something I put into action. Rather, my aim was to do things to my son-in-law that would annoy him, embarrass him, upset him, inconvenient him or simply make his life a little less happy – without him knowing that I was getting my revenge.

Some of the things that I did to my son-in-law, I wanted him to experience first hand. Some of the things, I wanted my daughter to experience or find before my son-in-law did so that he would need to explain to her why, when he had no possible explanation for those things. And other things, I just wanted to see, hear about or watch for myself, things that would make his life miserable.

Introduction

Some of the things in this book took a minute or less to put into action. Some things took a little bit longer. Some of these things required access to my daughter's home or to my son-in-law's car. And others were easily put into action from the comfort of my home, via the Internet.

It was pretty easy to set up some things when visiting my daughter at her home. For instance, I was able to *mess with* my son-in-law's clothes when she was on her phone. A gift certificate to a local spa for her birthday and offering to help her around the house when at the spa enabled me to do things that I couldn't do if she were there. For instance, I had a copy of their house key and the spare key to her husband's car cut, which opened doors enabling me to do more.

Some of the things I needed to get the job done:

- Hammer and a few nails
- Scissors
- Needle and some thread
- Super glue
- Hair dye
- Fresh baby, dog or cat poop
- Some cheap perfume and cologne
- Chewing gum
- Vegetable oil

- Petroleum jelly
- Clear fingernail polish
- A few garden slugs and snails (alive)
- A few bugs (alive and dead)
- Some disposable latex gloves
- A few prepaid credit cards
- A few disposable prepaid cell phones
- Laxatives
- A few raw shrimp
- A friend with a sexy voice
- The nerve and a sense of humor

The key to getting my *silent revenge* was that my son-in-law (and my daughter) had no idea that I was behind the things that happened to him. The reward was knowing that I had made my son-in-law's life a little less pleasant – without injuring or killing him or putting him (or me) in jail.

Revenge can be fun. It can also be dangerous. Accordingly, *everything* in this book comes with an important warning and disclaimer, provided on the following page. After you have read it, I hope that you enjoy my list of the 100 ways I got *Silent Revenge*.

Important

This book is strictly for entertainment purposes only. The contents of this book are *not* intended to be advice, suggestions or instructions on taking or on how to take revenge on anyone. The authors and publisher do not condone revenge.

Warning: Any person who chooses to carry out anything that appears in this book does so at **their own risk and takes full responsibility for their choices and actions and any and all results and consequences**.

Disclaimer: This book is sold with the full understanding that the authors and publisher **shall not be held liable or responsible** to any person or entity in any way with respect to, including but not limited to, any physical, psychological, emotional, commercial or financial (including business or employment) loss, injury, damage or costs or any interference, damage or loss to any current or future relationship incidentally or consequentially directly or indirectly caused, or alleged to have been caused, by anything contained within or in connection with this book or any of its content whatsoever.

PART 1
Keeping Him Clean

1

Use his toothbrush to clean the bathroom sink drain hole.

You *probably should* pull out any hair that might be stuck in his toothbrush after you've finished cleaning the hole, but after that, no cleaning is necessary. Simply return his toothbrush to the toothbrush holder. You may want to step on the toothbrush a few times before you do. (Ensure that your daughter hasn't used a drain cleaner or unclogger recently.)

2

Use his toothbrush to clean your toenails.

Imagine how nice it will feel when those toothbrush bristles tickle your toes and clean underneath your toe nails. You will also get an added bonus of knowing that every time he brushes his teeth, he will get a real taste of the pleasure your toes experienced.

3

Use his bath towel to clean the bathroom floor.

When finished cleaning the floor with his towel, there is no need to wash it. Simply let it hang dry. His towel may be a little hairy, as it's sure to have picked up some hair from the floor, but no problem. He may not notice or might simply think that it's hair that has rubbed off his manly body from the last shower or bath he had.

4

Put vegetable oil in his shampoo.

This is sure to leave his hair smooth and shiny. As his hair dries, it will be, look and feel greasy. It will also give his head a fry on a summer's day as the sun heats up the oil in his hair. (Of course, if your daughter and son-in-law use the same shampoo, you'll need to give this one a miss.)

5

Add hair dye to his shampoo.

Choose a color that closely matches the color of his shampoo so that he doesn't notice any difference in his shampoo. As many shampoos are yellow or green, his *new* hair color is sure to get a lot of attention. If he doesn't have much or any hair, put hair dye in his body wash. Over time, it might add a colorful tinge to his face, eyebrows and the top of his head. (If your son-in-law and daughter use the same body wash, you'll also need to give this one a miss.)

6

Use his comb or hair brush to comb or brush the family dog or cat.

If they don't have a dog or cat, maybe you can find a hairy stray dog or cat hanging around outside and give that dog or cat a nice comb or brush. The dog or cat is sure to enjoy that. (You *should probably* pick out any fleas or ticks that you see in the comb or brush – before taking it back inside.)

7

Break off half of the teeth in his comb or break off the handle of his hair brush.

If you're not into breaking things, you could put a small wad of chewed gum in his comb or brush. If your son-in-law has little or no hair on his bony head, you may still be in luck. If he has whiskers, a beard or a mustache, he may have a beard or mustache comb or brush that you could break for him or stick a wad of gum in.

8

Paint his bar of soap with clear finger nail polish.

Painting/covering his bar of soap with clear nail polish will prevent the soap from foaming up. This will result in a frustrating shower or bath. If he decides to use his shampoo (the shampoo in number 5 above) as a substitute for the useless bar of soap, his skin may have a nice colorful tone for the next few days.

Keeping Him Clean

9

Mess with his toothpaste tube.

Squeeze out about half of what's left in his tube of toothpaste into a bowl. (Keep a small amount of the toothpaste you squeeze out separately to later use as a plug for the tube.) Then mix the toothpaste with water so that the toothpaste has the consistency of tomato soup. Then pour the mixture back in the tube. (A kitchen funnel will make that easier.) Then cram some of the toothpaste that you saved separately into the tip of the tube. This acts as a plug – keeping the runny toothpaste in the tube until the dear son-in-law squeezes the tube the next time he brushes his teeth. (This is another one you probably want to pass on if your daughter and son-in-law use the same tube of toothpaste.)

10

Spray everything he uses to groom himself with something that smells really bad.

This would include things like his soap and face towel, electric shaver or razor and shave cream can or tube, deodorant stick or spray can, hair spray or gel or mousse tube or container, head wax tin, comb or brush, and toothbrush and toothpaste tube. (You may be able to find something that stinks really bad, such as novelty fart spray, in a gag store or on Amazon.)

PART 2
His Car

11

Let the air out of this car tires – once every three months for a year.

There is nothing like a flat tire (or four) when rushing off to work or going to a sporting event. Letting the air out of two or more tires will definitely ruin his day. (Not many people keep more than one spare inflated tire in their car.)

12

Put fresh moist baby or dog poop under the driver's seat of his car.

Summer is a real winner for this one. Heat and rolled up windows brings out the best of any poop. Your son-in-law is sure to smell it when he gets in his car. There is also a chance that he may stick his hand into the poop as he probes under the car seat in search of the source of the smell.

13

If he drives a car to work, wet the driver's seat.

You don't need to pee on his seat (though that could leave a nice smelly wet spot, that if lucky just might leave a stain). Any liquid should do the trick. If the seats happen to be a dark color, he might not see the wet spot. If things go as planned, he might not even notice the wetness until after he is on his way to work. And, depending on what liquid you use (ink verses water, for instance), there may be a nice stain on the back side of his pants for all to see when he gets to work.

14

Put a raw shrimp under the driver's seat of his car.

Like number 12, summer is a great time for this one. The rotting shrimp will quickly give off a nice smell for him to suck in when driving to work. The smell will likely cling to his clothes, following him around all day. The smell is also likely to remain in the car's air conditioner for weeks, maybe even months. This could mean, no air conditioner for the rest of the summer.

15

When in his or their family car, stick your finger down your throat and throw up on the back seat.

A good barf in the car will smell really bad and is sure to stick around for months. And chances are, it will likely be your dear son-in-law who will be the one to have to clean it up.

16

Stick your finger down your throat and barf all over the hood of his car.

Barfing on the hood of your son-in-law's car is a great way to start your (and his) day. Eating a big spaghetti with corn meal before barfing will provide an extra touch. If you wish to leave a memory of that day, do your barfing on a hot sunny day when your son-in-law is sick in bed with the flu. Doing so will give the sun time to bake the barf onto the hood of his car.

17

Shove fresh dog poop under the door handle on the driver's side of his car.

This is when those latex gloves come in handy. He is sure to get a nice surprise when he opens his car door – as he, unlike you, won't be wearing gloves.

18

Put some fresh dog poop on the hood of his car.

The poop you use will make a big difference. With the hard type, a big bird might pick it up and fly away with it or it might simply roll off the hood. You want the moist type, the type that looks like twisting soft serve ice cream. Again, if done in the summer, the heat is likely to bake the poop onto his car – nice and hard.

19

Spread petroleum jelly on the windscreen of his car.

Ensure that you leave a 12 inch petroleum jelly free circle on the driver's side in the event that he doesn't take the time to wipe off the windshield. The 12 inch circle should enable him to see just enough to drive. (You may want him dead but you don't want to kill him.) If he tries to wipe it off, he's likely to make a bigger mesh, smearing the petroleum jelly all over the windshield. This should stop him from driving his car at least until he uses soap and water to do a proper job.

20

Stick an odd or stupid bumper sticker on his car's back bumper.

A bumper sticker with something like:
- "Honk if you're horny" or
- "Mine is bigger than yours"

should do the trick. Use super glue to attach the sticker to his car bumper. This will mean that it won't be a simple peel it off job for him. Better if he needs to spend a good part of his day off to scrub and rub to get the sticker off the bumper. This is sure to piss him off for weeks wondering who stuck it on his car.

PART 3
Clothes Make the Man

21

Put some fresh baby, dog or cat poop in his jacket or coat pocket.

The wet, soft and sticky kind works best. It may be that he doesn't put his hand in that pocket straight away. That's OK, as the smell is sure to get worse as the day or evening progresses. He is likely to eventually check his pockets for the source of the smell.

22

Sew or apply super glue to the toe area of his favorite socks.

When he tries to put his socks on, the stitched or super glued area will prevent him from doing so. If he doesn't have or you don't know which socks are his favorites, you could stitch or super glue his sports socks or a few pairs of the socks he wears to work.

23

Stick chewed gum on the bottom of his shoes.

His work, casual or sports shoes, even his house slippers will do fine. No one likes having to pick off chewed gum from the bottom of their shoes (or slippers). If you are lucky, he won't notice the gum stuck on the bottom of his shoes or house slippers straight away. Chances are that if he doesn't notice it, the gum will have also stuck to the carpet of his car or in the bedroom or living room carpet at home.

24

If his work shoes have laces, cut half of both laces just below the top eyelet so the laces will break when he pulls them tight to tie his shoes.

Unlikely that he'll have an extra pair of laces at home. If he doesn't have another pair of work shoes, he'll need to tie the broken laces together.

25

Put itching powder in his underwear.

This is sure to have him frantically itching his balls in public until he can get home to change his undies. This works best if your son-in-law wears briefs/jockey style underwear rather than boxers, as the powder will stay in there all day long. (Gag stores often sell itching powder. Or you might wish to make your own. Evidently, crushed rose hips or maple tree seed pods will do the trick.)

26

Wash his socks and fold or roll them when they are still wet.

You might also want to wash all of his favorite weekend shirts (aren't you nice) and rather than dry or hang them up, wad them up into a ball while still wet and put them in his shirt drawer or toss them in the wardrobe or closet. This may lead to a quarrel with his wife about her recent laundry skills. When she rightfully defends herself, since she wasn't the one who did it, it may put him in the dog house for the night.

27

Sew up part of the neck hole of his favorite turtle neck shirt or sweater so that his fat head doesn't fit through.

Sew just enough so that he can almost get his head in. You want him to struggle with getting that fat thing in the neck hole. Imagine his frustration and confusion as he tries to put it into the hole.

28

After you take a poop – wipe your butt with his work tie or one of his socks.

Naturally, a dark neck tie or sock is best. But in a pinch, a nice bum smear on a lightly colored tie or sock may have to do. If he sees it or gets a whiff when he puts on his tie or socks, that's OK as he may take it up with his wife then or when he gets home from work. If he doesn't see the smear or notice the smell, chances are others at work will.

29

Super glue one of his work shoes to the floor.

Not only will he be annoyed at having to try to peel his shoe off the floor, he will likely have to clean up left over pieces of his shoe heel off the floor when he gets home from work.

30

Cut some of the seams in the crouch of his favorite pants.

Cut just enough so that the seams in the crouch of his pant will split *after* he leaves home. The aim is that his pant's crouch seams split enough so that his underwear will be visible for all to see. If he is wearing boxers or loose underpants, maybe his balls will hang out and a big dog will mistake them for a treat and take a bite.

31

Put a few living cockroaches in his underwear drawer.

Wrap the live cockroaches in the crotch of a few pairs of his underwear. The critters will probably like the warmth and darkness of your son-in-law's underwear, so much so that they may wish to set up house and start a large family. No man likes to be met by a cockroach or two when putting on his undies. An added bonus, when the cockroaches die, their crunchy little bodies will stick onto his undies. Dead crunchy cockroach bodies are sure to make his underwear rather uncomfortable.

32

Pry/loosen a heel of his work or dress shoes.

Pry or loosen a heel so that the heel will stay on just long enough for him to walk out the door. This would be inconvenient for him at the least if the shoes were the only dress shoes he owns. It could be catastrophic if he's on his way out to attend an important event or meeting. Imagine the big smile on your face if you later hear from your daughter that the son-in-law had to wear his sports shoes with his suit.

33

Put a live snail or garden slug in his pant's pocket.

These critters tend to leave a *slime* trail wherever they are. While both do the job, slugs are better than snails since there is a chance that your son-in-law might touch the hard snail shell when he puts is hand in his pocket rather than the moist squishy slug body. If you aren't able to find a juicy snail or slug in your garden, you might be able to buy a few at your local pet store.

34

Hammer a small nail into the sole of one of his shoes.

Find, borrow or buy a nail that is long enough to just penetrate the insole of his shoe. (Do not use a rusty nail.) You want the pointy end of the nail to stick out inside his shoe just enough to prick him when he walks. The nail head should be flat so that it is more difficult for him to spot if he looks at the bottom of his shoe to find what is poking him.

35

If he has insoles in his shoes, remove one of the insoles and hide it under the sofa.

Like extra shoes laces, he's unlikely to have an extra insole to replace the one that *mysteriously* disappeared. If he uses insoles to make him look taller, a missing insole in one of his shoes is sure to make him look a bit lopsided. And if he uses insoles for comfort, he's likely to be uncomfortable when wearing those shoes, until he buys a new set of insoles.

36

Create a stain on one of his favorite shirts.

A splash of grape juice, red wine, coffee, ink or a rub of a hand full of grass from outside is sure to leave a nice long lasting stain. If your daughter can't get the stain out, her good old husband will need to spend some of his hard earned cash to buy a new favorite shirt.

PART 4
Get Him Where He Lives

37

Put something sticky under the toilet seat where he would put his fingers to pick up the seat to pee.

Peanut butter, strawberry jam or maple syrup should do fine. If they have a baby, dog or cat, you might consider using some freshly pooped poop.

38

Pee on the toilet seat.

A nice squirt of pee on the toilet seat never goes unnoticed. Even guys who squirt on their own toilet seats at home don't enjoy wiping pee off if they need to take a poop. If your daughter uses the toilet before he does and spots the pee, she's likely to blame him, as she knows you sit when you pee.

39

Pee in his favorite coffee mug.

Let the pee sit in there for about 10 minutes then pour out the pee. But, of course, don't wash the mug after you pour out the pee. (If you are up for a dare, you could leave a little bit of pee in the mug to dry naturally.)

40

Fart on his pillow.

The more farts that you can pump out on and into his pillow the merrier. This one can be performed often. You simply need to have access to his pillow. You might want to vary what you eat the night before so to provide your son-in-law with a bit of variety. For instance, you might eat a large bowl of Sauerkraut one night, a big plate of Mexican re-fired beans another, and maybe a bucket of Brussels sprouts on the night before his birthday. (You need to be strong for this one as it requires that you hold it all in until you get to their house the following morning to let it all out onto his pillow. If your holding ability isn't strong, *especially* with the Brussels sprouts, you may need to eat these things for breakfast then quickly get in your car and make a quick dash to your daughter's house.)

41

Mess with his shaver or razor so that he is unable to shave for work on Monday morning.

If you do this on Sunday, he probably will not notice until or have the time to buy a new razor before Monday morning. If he uses an electric shaver, you could throw out the battery in his shaver and hide the AC adapter. If he uses one of those twin or triple blade type razors, you might stick chewed gum between the blades.

42

Hide all of their toilet paper including the roll on the toilet paper holder.

Nothing nicer for a man after a poop than to find that there is no toilet paper. This is especially true if there is no one home to get him a roll while he waits. If your daughter is first to use the toilet, she's likely to blame her inconsiderate husband for not replacing the toilet paper.

43

Put laxative in his coffee creamer.

If he drinks his coffee black or your daughter also uses creamer in her coffee, you might consider buying some laxative that looks like pieces of real chocolate (Often sold in gag stores.) This is assuming that he likes chocolate, of course. If your daughter *also* likes chocolate, well, chances are she probably needs her pipes cleaned anyway.

44

Leave a big poop in the toilet for him to find.

If your daughter happens to find it first, she is likely to blame your son-in-law, as she is sure that you would never leave things that way. If your poop really smells and your daughter is at home, you may want to leave this one for another day. Or, rather than use your own, you could use dog poop, either their dog's or that which you bring with you. You may be able to find some fresh dog poop on someone's lawn that you could scoop up and take with you to your daughter's home.

45

Wipe your butt with his pillow case.

Naturally, as with all butt wiped neck ties and socks, a dark colored pillow case works best. He (and your daughter) is less likely to notice the wipe until he puts his ugly face on his pillow. If they don't already have a set of dark colored pillow cases, maybe you could give them a set of chocolate brown bed sheets with matching pillow cases for Christmas next year.

46

Wet his side of the bed.

Pour some water or other liquid of your choice on his side of the bed. Doing this in the winter can provide even more satisfaction, as it would be very cold when he gets into bed. If you're up to it, you might squat and pee on his side of the bed, aiming for the area of his side of the bed where his back or stomach would be. If you feel like giving him a little bonus, simply walk over to his pillow before you're finished doing your business and give it a squirt.

47

Put a few garden variety slugs and snails in his underwear drawer.

Not only will the slug and snail slime leave a nice sticky feel to the inside of his undies, they may set up house in some of his underwear. They will also leave small poops all around the inside his underwear. You might need to bring some lettuce with you occasionally to feed them so that they don't die or leave to find somewhere else to live.

48

Obscure his face in family photos in their home.

You might consider spilling something on his face in a photo, obstructing it with something like a stuffed toy or other photo, or even cutting his face out of the photo. (If your daughter and son-in-law have a child, chances are they will think their child did the cutting.) The aim is to give the creep a creepy feeling when he sees that his face is covered or missing in the family photos.

49

If he drinks beer or fizzy soda, vigorously shake all the cans and bottles in their fridge right before he's due home.

If you're lucky, the beer or soda will explode in his face when he opens the cans or bottles. Not only will he have beer or fizzy soda all over himself, hopefully he (not your daughter) will need to clean it off the walls and ceilings.

50

If he drinks beer or fizzy soda, put all cans that are in the refrigerator into the freezer and then put them back in the refrigerator when you leave.

Frozen and puffy cans of beer and fizzy soda have little purpose or value in life. Just like him.

51

In the summer, take all of his beer or soda out of the refrigerator.

Friday is likely the best time for this one. There is nothing nicer than a warm beer or soda when he has been thinking about a cold one when he gets home from work. If he doesn't have one on Friday, he's *sure to* want one when he sits down to watch sports on TV on Saturday afternoon or when he's out in the yard.

52

Put a bug in some of his favorite food.

Discover what foods he likes but your daughter doesn't eat and stick a juicy bug or two in that food. The choice is yours whether the bugs are dead or alive. This is something that you can do as often as you please. Potato salad is great for this one. Simply stick a small bug or two into a chunk of potato. If they have a bean salad in their refrigerator, this too will work fine. If you can't find the right bug, a few worms will work nicely with pretty much any food.

53

Put a wad of hair in something he likes to eat when he gets home from work.

After a hard day at work, your son-in-law is probably thinking about how nice it will be to grab a snack and sit down to watch some TV when he gets home. A wad of hair in his food is sure to destroy that pleasure. You're sure to find an assortment of hair in the bathroom sink. A curly pubic hair can add that extra touch. (Be sure your daughter doesn't also like the targeted food.)

54

Stuff one of his socks down the toilet so that it backs up the next time someone flushes the toilet.

Timing is important here. You want to do this just before your son-in-law is due to get home and just as you are leaving their home. If you get a chance, do a big poop in the toilet *before* you stuff the sock in it. This is sure to be a nice surprise. If your daughter uses the toilet before he does, she's likely to ask him to deal with the mess as soon as he walks in the door.

55

Pee on the floor in front of the toilet so that he steps in your pee when he uses the toilet.

As with all toilet tricks, you need to perform this just before your son-in-law gets home and just as you are leaving their home. Like many of us, he's likely to want to take a pee as soon as he walks in the door. In the event that your daughter uses the toilet before he does, and she happens to step in your pee, chances are pretty good that she will blame her husband (or child or pet if they have one) for the pee.

56

Spray something on this pillow that stinks really bad.

A good butt wipe on his pillow case (see #45) is sure to leave a nice smell. However, to keep the good times rolling in, don't stop with a simple butt wipe. Go all out. Find a nasty smelling substance and spray or smear it on his pillow. The nasty smell could stick around for a few weeks. The smell might even seep deep into the pillow making it impossible to get rid of the smell. This may mean even more of your son-in-law's hard earned cash is spent, to buy another pillow.

57

When you have a cold or the flu, cough and sneeze on his pillow.

The more "juice" you can cough or sneeze onto his pillow the better the chances are that he'll get a cold or the flu soon after. If you have the energy and are up to it, you could also cough and sneeze into his favorite coffee mug. It's nice to share.

58

If he has an allergy, put some of the substance that triggers his allergy in or on his pillow.

It may be as simple as putting a bit of cat or dog fur inside his pillow case. Or maybe shaking a dust cloth full of dust mites or sprinkling a few bits of pollen on his pillow. Whatever you use, it's *very important* to make sure that his allergy isn't the kind of allergy that could send him to the hospital or could kill him.

PART 5
Get Him Where He Works.

59

Spray a really cheap cologne on his work shirts.

He might not notice it but his co-workers and boss will. He's sure to get at least frowns of disapproval from some at work. Some may label him a loser, which as far as you are concerned, he is. Others may take him aside to tell him that he needs to back off the cologne. If he works only with other men, his cologne is sure to raise a few eyebrows maybe even get a few winks. A good time to put this one into action is when he has a cold. Chances are his nose won't be working right and thus might not be able to smell the cologne.

60

Put a leaky pen in his work pants or shirt pocket.

If he works at a job that requires a clean pressed dress shirt and or pants, for instance, an office manager, a nice ink stain could ruin his day. If he's an overalls or uniform kind of guy, an ink stain might not go unnoticed by management. Whatever he wears, if you're lucky, the ink will *leak through* his shirt, pants, overalls or uniform and leave a nice ink stain on his crusty body.

61

Add his name, work phone and email address to spam lists and junk websites.

We all love to get junk phone calls and emails. It's always great fun to spend our valuable time filtering out junk phone calls and email – totally useless and irrelevant crap. Spending a few of your hours adding his details to every website you can find that offers useless junk or stuff that he has no interest in could result in months of time wasting effort on his part to stop the emails and calls from coming. That could be months of *pleasure for you* and months of misery for him.

62

Spray a really horrible smelling substance on all of his work shirts.

As with a cheap cologne, a nasty smelling co-worker is a nightmare for other co-workers, and bosses. Sundays are best for this one as your son-in-law and daughter are unlikely to notice the smell until Monday morning when he's getting ready to go to work. This could mean that there wouldn't be time for him or your daughter to wash his shirts before he needs to leave for work. (A good fart spray (#10) would work nicely here.)

63

Order online six cases of cheap whiskey and have it delivered to him at his work place.

Set up an account with an online liquor store in his name, providing his work place phone and address. Then order the cheapest whiskey they offer. Make sure that the cases are sent as is, not wrapped. You want everyone at his work place to see the contents of the cases when delivered and when sitting at his desk or in his office. You will need to pay for it when you order and you don't want the order in your name. This is the time to use one of your prepaid credit cards.

64

Make some prank calls to him when he is at work.

Have a friend help you with this one. Chances are no matter how hard you try to disguise your voice, your son-in-law would likely recognize your voice. Have your friend use one of the pre-paid cell phones you bought before you started this project. You could have your friend call him at work and tell him that she's selling the new *Mr. Monster Dick* penis enlargement pump, for instance. If he's out of the office or away from his phone, be sure she leaves a loud message on his phone or answering machine. If he works at a company that has a receptionist, be sure that your friend leaves a message, mentioning your son-in-law's name and what she's selling.

65

Send a letter to his boss asking his boss for a job reference for your son-in-law.

Computers and printers today give anyone the ability to create company stationary (paper with a company logo and address and matching envelopes). If you don't have the needed skills to do so, chances are someone you know does. Write a short letter to your son-in-law's boss (on the created stationary) from a competitor asking for a job reference regarding your son-in-law. From that day forward, his boss may treat him differently and may confront him on the issue.

66

Contact companies to send pamphlets to him at his work place advertising creams and drugs to treat nasty health conditions.

The Internet is filled with websites advertising creams and cures for nasty things, like herpes and sexually transmitted diseases. Contact them online and ask for information and samples to be sent in his name to his work address.

67

Contact a drug user helpline and tell them that a friend needs help.

Even if your son-in-law does not have a drug problem, he does have a problem, that is – You Hate Him and he needs help. Ask them to send information to your "friend" at his work place and provide them with your son-in-law's name and work address. If the person who answers the helpline asks for your name, tell them that you wish to remain anonymous.

68

Contact a cheesy escort service and ask for an escort to be sent to your son-in-law's work place and for her to ask for him by his first name.

Find the cheapest place in town with the ugliest and oldest escorts. Ask them to send an *older lady* who wears a lot of make-up. Teeth optional.

69

Call and ask an *unconventional* group to send members to his work place to speak with your son-in-law.

Regardless of your son-in-law's interest in new ideas, a visit from any non-work related group at work during work hours is sure to annoy his boss. A bonus if the members show up wearing odd costumes or hairstyles or have pointy ears.

70

Change the time on his alarm clock at home so that he's late for work the following day.

A Tuesday or Wednesday may be the best day to reset his alarm clock. He's unlikely to check the time set on his alarm clock on a Tuesday or Wednesday night since his alarm went off as usual (the time he had set it to go off) on Monday and Tuesday morning.

71

Get a friend pretending to be *Humpy's Escort Service* to call your son-in-law's boss regarding getting paid for the son-in-law's outstanding $6500 balance.

Chances are his boss will not be impressed.

72

Put crewed gum in his work pants' front pockets.

Probably five or six crewed sticks of gum will do the job. You want the gum to stick to everything he puts in his pocket. Sticky gum on his car keys, wallet and fingers is sure to make his day.

PART 6
Embarrass and Inconvenience Him

73

When with the family, sit near him and fart as often as you can – and blame him for the farts.

The smellier and louder the better. As soon as you have released a big one, get up and move away from him and say something like – *Come on Bill, stop farting*.

74

Get someone to call his cell phone at about 3 am on a work night.

When he answers, the caller might do some or all of the following:

- Breath heavily
- Say nothing
- Fart in the phone
- Ask him if he wants a date

Maybe you know someone who works the very earlier morning shift. Or maybe you could pay someone who does. A homeless gal or one who walks the streets at night may be willing to help you out for a few bucks and a prepaid phone.

75

Put an alarm clock near his side of the bed set to go off at 3 or 4 am.

Better yet, set two different alarms for different times, such as 3 am and 4 am. Put one near his side of the bed and another in a room that's close enough for him to hear it when it goes off. This is sure to also disturb your daughter's sleep. But if she were you, she would probably feel that it was well worth a disrupted night or two of sleep.

76

Cancel his favorite sports and or on-demand movie streaming service.

If his login details have been saved in his computer browser or are written down somewhere, this might be as simple as doing it online. If you are required to call to cancel, you could get a male friend to make the call pretending to be your son-in-law. Of course, you could call pretending to be your daughter. If he were to call the streaming service company to find out who canceled the service and if he were to accuse your daughter of canceling his service, that may put your son-in-law back in the dog house for a night or two.

77

Post ads and fliers on supermarket ad boards for free smart phones – and include his name and cell phone number.

This is sure to confuse and annoy him. He may even need to deal with irate *customers* when he tells them that they have the wrong number. These calls could go on for months or at least until he finds and takes down all ads and fliers.

78

When out for a meal with your daughter's family, chew with your mouth open so food falls out.

Not much your son-in-law can do about you allowing the food in your mouth fall out onto your clothes or the table. He may try to exclude you from future family outings but your daughter is unlikely to allow him to do it. (Especially if she doesn't see food fall out of your mouth when out with the family.)

79

Add his email address to mailing lists on porn and sex toys websites.

He is sure to be happy to find all those goodies quickly filling up his email in-box. If you really want to be nasty, then be sure to include his full (real) name and office mailing address. (Be sure to use a VPN or public computer when visiting these sites so that they don't get a hold of your details. You don't want this kind of stuff in your email in-box.)

80

Advertise his car for sale at a really cheap price in the local newspaper or online.

In addition to his cell phone, be sure to include his work phone number so that he gets a lot of calls when at home, at work and during his free time. He's sure to be irritated with the calls and having to tell callers that his car is not for sale. He may have to deal with claims of false advertising and people who threaten to sue him or worse. And if you're lucky, all the calls at work may get him into trouble with his boss.

81

Call sales people and get strangers to come to his home at 8 am on Sunday.

You're sure to find carpet and curtain cleaning companies more than happy to come over and give your son-in-law a demonstration and free quote. You could put an ad in the newspaper advertising a Sunday 8 am garage sale or open house at their home. Or how about a free car wash in their yard starting at 8. These are sure to excite eager early rising bargain hunters from near and far. Their knocks on the door will be a great start to your son-in-law's Sunday. Best time for this one is when you have asked your daughter to stay Saturday night at your place.

82

When in public with his family, ask him embarrassing questions.

This is for those times when your daughter is out of hearing range (for instance, when she is using the restroom) but others can clearly hear what you are asking him. It could be asking him if he's still unable to *get it up* (if he is impotent). It may be asking him if his hemorrhoids are still bothering him. Or maybe it's asking him if he has sorted out his itchy balls problem or if his diarrhea has cleared up. He doesn't need to have any of these issues to ask – does he.

83

"Borrow" his cell phone for a few days.

This one might be a tough one to pull off. It's likely that you will need to take his cell phone when he is at home. Maybe one day when you are visiting your daughter and the son-in-law is outside working in the yard or is glued to the TV, you could slip his phone into your purse. Naturally, you don't want his cell phone to ring when it's in your purse. So you will need to do this one just before leaving their home. Imagine our son-in-law frantically looking for his missing cell phone. If you want to be really nasty, you could mess with his phone when you are *borrowing* it.

84

Sign him up to receive heaps of junk in the mail.

The Internet is filled with websites offering all kinds of junk that's available for free delivery to the home. Maybe it's samples of vaginal cream, free videos on how to use a penis enlargement device or breast pump or it may be information about time-share condos in Laos or Mongolia. Be creative. You want stuff to be sent to your son-in-law that he has absolutely no interest in. You could also order stuff that isn't free and would be sent as pay-on-delivery or pay later.

PART 7
Trouble With The Wife

☠ WARNING ☠

What follows can destroy relationships, including yours with your daughter.

85

Order Suzy the sex doll for him to be delivered to the home while he is at work.

It might be best to use a prepaid use only once type of credit card when ordering Suzy. When you order her, be sure to arrange for her to be delivered when the son-in-law definitely won't be at home. You want your daughter to be the one to receive Suzy. When your son-in-law gets home, your daughter will surely have questions about Miss Suzy's arrival. It's pretty likely that your son-in-law and Miss Suzy will be sharing the sofa that night – or sleeping in the car.

86

Buy one or two pornographic DVDs and hide them under the mattress on his side of the bed.

Ensure that when you stick the DVDs under the mattress that just enough is visible so that your daughter will find them. If your son-in-law has pornographic stuff visible in the house and your daughter is OK with it, then you should skip this one. Bringing more porn into their home is only going to add to his happiness, which, of course, is not your aim.

87

Sign him up on various dating websites.

Create a profile with juicy details (lies). Include things like he: volunteers at a local orphanage, drives a Ferrari or Lamborghini and that he's in the $500,000+ a year income bracket. Be sure to include his cell phone number and email. And, of course, you'll need a nice photo of your son-in-law to include with his profile. You're sure to find photos on the Internet of great looking guys with sufficient muscles and a shaved chest to attract the ladies. The hotter looking that guy is the more phone calls and emails your son-in-law is going to get – interrupting his day and night and having to explain to his wife why he is getting calls and emails from other women.

88

Send him a "love" letter to his home.

A short note with a few drawn hearts and even a lip stick kiss on the letter should do the trick. Put the letter in a fancy *feminine* envelop. Before sealing the envelop, take the letter to a cosmetic counter at your local department store and give it a big squirt of one of the perfume samples. You may wish to go all out on this one and send him a "love gift." That could be something like home baked cookies or a handmade wool penis sock. Be sure you write a woman's name on the return address so that your daughter just can't stop herself from opening the package.

89

Buy him a Cross-Dresser magazine subscription and have it sent to him at his home.

This will be a tough one for him to explain to his wife. If they haven't been married for long, he may have a tough time proving to his wife that he didn't order the subscription. A potential bonus for you could be that by ordering him a subscription to this magazine, his details could be sold or given to other magazines and businesses selling *unique* goods and services. Your initial efforts here may lead to things being sent to him that he could never explain to his wife.

90

Buy a few naked women magazines and "hide" them under the bathroom sink.

As with #86, if your daughter is OK with naked women magazines, this one is best skipped. If she isn't a fan of her husband looking at naked women in magazines, then this could land him yet again in the dog house.☺ Like #86, ensure that just enough of one of the magazine covers (a boob or two) is visible so your daughter will find them (before her husband does).

91

Have a female friend call your son-in-law at 10 or 11 at night.

The sexier your friend's voice is the better. Just ask her to pretend to be one of his girlfriends. Also tell her to be sure to speak loudly so that your daughter will hear a female voice. Unless your son-in-law is a total dickhead and wants to talk with the woman on the phone, he's likely to hang up quickly. So get your friend to say a few nasty or sexy things on the phone before he hangs up.

92

Sign him up for a year subscription to a sex toys magazine to be sent to his home.

This would be a tough one for him to explain to his wife if she isn't into toys. But at the same time, it could back fire on you. Your son-in-law and daughter might find some of the sex toys offered in the magazines exciting and order a few to give them a try. Always keep in mind – his joy and pleasure are not on your agenda.

93

Order him a big rubber dildo from an Internet store.

Choose pay-on-delivery and organize for it to be delivered when your daughter will be home to *receive* it. The address on the package is likely to give her a good idea of what's inside. If you are lucky, she will open it before her husband gets home. This one too may backfire, however. Without you knowing it, your daughter may play with the thing and keep it for herself.

94

Order flowers to be delivered to him at his home.

Red roses are probably the best choice here. Be sure to have the florist include a nice card. Ask the florist to write a message in the card. Something such as, *Had a great time the other night* or something more to the point, like, *I miss your sausage,* should do the trick. Be sure to ask the florist to sign the card with something corny or stupid like, *Your muffin* or *Your love tunnel.*

95

Mess with his home computer.

If you have computer skills, you might change his computer desktop wallpaper to a photo of a naked man or woman, for instance. You might create a new desktop shortcut link to the online store where you bought that rubbery dildo in #93. You could also add some new links to his favorites list on his browser, such as links to a pornographic website or store selling inflatables (men and women blow up dolls). For this one to work, it's best if your daughter also uses his (the same) computer at home. You want your daughter to see the nice additions and changes you've made to his computer *before* your son-in-law has the chance to change or delete the changes you made.

96

Send him a box of chocolates on Valentine's Day.

Include a note signed "from a secret admirer." If you think chocolates are too cliché and wish to be a little more creative, you could find and pay a strange woman (or man) to do a dance, record it on your phone, copy it to a DVD, wrap it then send it to his home. Or maybe send him a pair of underwear, the kind with a round hole in the front for a man's hose to hang out. Like in #88, if you give the package a few squirts of perfume, your daughter may open the package to have a look before her husband gets home.

97

Get a friend to call his home pretending to be one of his past lovers.

Get your friend to call your son-in-law's home when he definitely will not be there so that your daughter answers the phone. Have your friend say that she's an ex lover in town for the weekend hoping to *connect*. Or better yet, if you have a feminine male friend, have him call. Have him say something like, "Is this his mother" or "Is BJ home?" Get someone who can create and carry on a sex filled lie in the event his wife probes to find out more about her husband's *past lovers*.

98

Put a note with a phone number and woman's name in one of his pants' pockets.

Write something, like *Call me*, on a small piece of paper. The back side of a gum wrapper works nicely. (Looks spontaneous.) Be sure to include a phone number (your choice, a brothel might be nice) and a woman's name. Next time you are at their home and you see a pair of his pants in their laundry basket, slip that note into one of the pockets. If luck is with you, your daughter will find the note when she checks the pockets before she does the laundry.

99

Stuff a sexy lace bra in one of his pants' pockets.

Be prepared for the opportunity. Buy a cheap bra (red or black lace or imitation leather will do nicely) the next time you're at a discount store. Or maybe one of your friends has one laying around that she no longer uses. Next time you see a pair of his pants in their laundry basket, stuff that baby deep inside one of the pockets. If your daughter has even basic laundry skills, she is sure to notice something in the pocket and will pull it out before doing the laundry.

100

Put a little bit of lipstick on one of his shirt collars.

The next time you see one of his shirts in their laundry basket, simply pull out that lipstick and do your thing. You'll need to ensure that it's a color or shade that neither you or your daughter use. Chances are your daughter will see the lipstick mark(s) when she does the laundry. If you wish to be really mean and nasty, put a little bit of lipstick in the right places on a few pairs of his underwear.

Epilogue

Life can be cruel. You spend 18 years or more of your life raising an intelligent, considerate and well mannered daughter. But for some reason, you end up with a loser, an idiot, a real dickhead son-in-law. It happened to me. For me, I was left with only three choices. One was to totally ignore him. That wasn't going to work as he lived with my daughter. Another option was to put up with him. That too wasn't possible as he is such a loser. The third option was to get revenge.

I never let on to my daughter that I hated her husband so much. I smiled a lot whenever I was near him and when my daughter and I spoke of him. And I was so friendly to him that he and my daughter probably thought that he was my best friend. This enabled me to throw off any suspicion that I was behind the terrible things happening to my dear son-in-law.

My well played out *silent revenge* didn't change my son-in-law. He's still an idiot and I still hate him. However, it did make his life a little less pleasant, sometimes even outright miserable. In fact, even today he and my daughter still talk about some of the things that happened to him.

I'm lucky that no one knows (except you) that I was behind it all. Some of the things I did could have ended very badly, which thankfully they didn't. Looking back on it all, it provided me a sense of justice, and that makes me happy.

May your son-in-law be a real angel.

If you enjoyed this book, your review on Amazon or a nice comment on Facebook or other social media sites or blogs would certainly be most appreciated.

Other books from Simple Logic Publications. Available on Amazon and on other online book sellers' websites:

Ever wonder if *you might be a Dickhead*? Maybe you aren't really sure what makes someone a Dickhead. Or maybe you aren't a Dickhead but you know someone who is, someone who does not know that they are in fact a Dickhead, and you want them to know that they are.

If so, this book is for you.

Are You A Dickhead? asks the reader 100 simple questions and provides simple multiple choice answers. By answering the questions, the reader is able to generate a score. This score enables the reader to determine if they are or are not in fact a Dickhead.

From inside *Are You A Dickhead?*

When in public, do you: (Question 1)

R Pick your nose and look at what you picked.
U Pick your nose and flick whatever you picked out into the air.
A Pick your nose only when you know for sure that no one is looking or watching.
D Pick your nose and eat what you have picked out.
H Pick your nose and put what you picked out into your pocket to eat later.

When riding on a plane, train, bus or subway, do you: (Question 34)

R Stink (have BO) or reek of garlic.
U Allow your body to lean onto someone you don't know who is seated next to you.
A Fall asleep on the shoulder of someone you don't know who is sitting next to you.
D Sit with your mouth wide open, snore or drool, or all of the above.
H Smell kind of nice, allow the person sitting next to you to have and use their space by keeping your body parts in your part of your seat, and always ensure that your mouth doesn't hang open and that you don't snore or drool.

Do the people you think are *friends* do or fail to do things that you expect a friend to not do or to do? Does it seem like they have forgotten what it means to be a *friend*? Or could it be that they don't have a clue what it takes to be a friend?

Do some of your *friends* get irritated, even upset with you for things you do or don't do? Could it be that *you* have forgotten or don't *really know* what it means or takes to be a friend?

If so, this book is for them, and you.

This book takes a fun but serious look at what *real friends* do. It looks at things that make someone a real friend, things like: accepting us for who we really are, and telling us if we have a booger hanging out of your nose – when we do.

From inside *What Friends SHOULD Do*

Friends tell their friends if they have a big honking zit on their face. (No. 1)

The same applies to boogers hanging out of our nose, bad breath, body odor and things stuck in between our teeth or hanging out of our mouth. A real friend wouldn't let their friend walk around all day or night wondering why people are looking at or pointing at them – unaware of any freaky or smelly stuff that is sticking out of or coming from their body. A real friend will let us know immediately if they notice something that needs our attention (things like zits, boogers, or B.O.).

Friends help friends find solutions to their problems. (No. 29)

A real friend is there and ready to help a friend with a problem. It may be a problem a friend recognizes on their own. Or it might be something a friend sees in a friend that the friend doesn't see themselves. Either way, a real friend doesn't attack a friend with nasty comments but rather *attacks the problem* (helps find a solution). A real friend is only interested in helping their friend work out their problem. For instance: if a friend is really overweight, a real friend doesn't call that friend gigantor or chunky. A real friend would organize time with that friend to exercise together, to lose weight. If a friend loses their job, a real friend won't call the friend a loser. A real friend helps their friend to determine why they lost their job and what they can do to get another job.

www.ingramcontent.com/pod-product-compliance
Lightning Source LLC
Chambersburg PA
CBHW050434010526
44118CB00013B/1524